AF292198

Tale of Lakewood Jenny

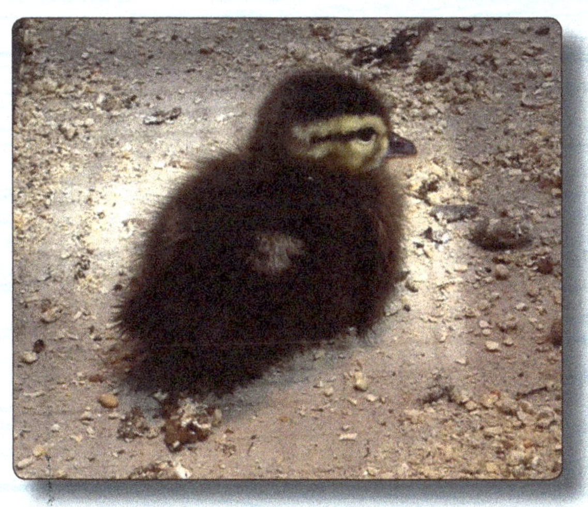

A true story about a wood duck

by

Jackie Caswell

Lakewood Books

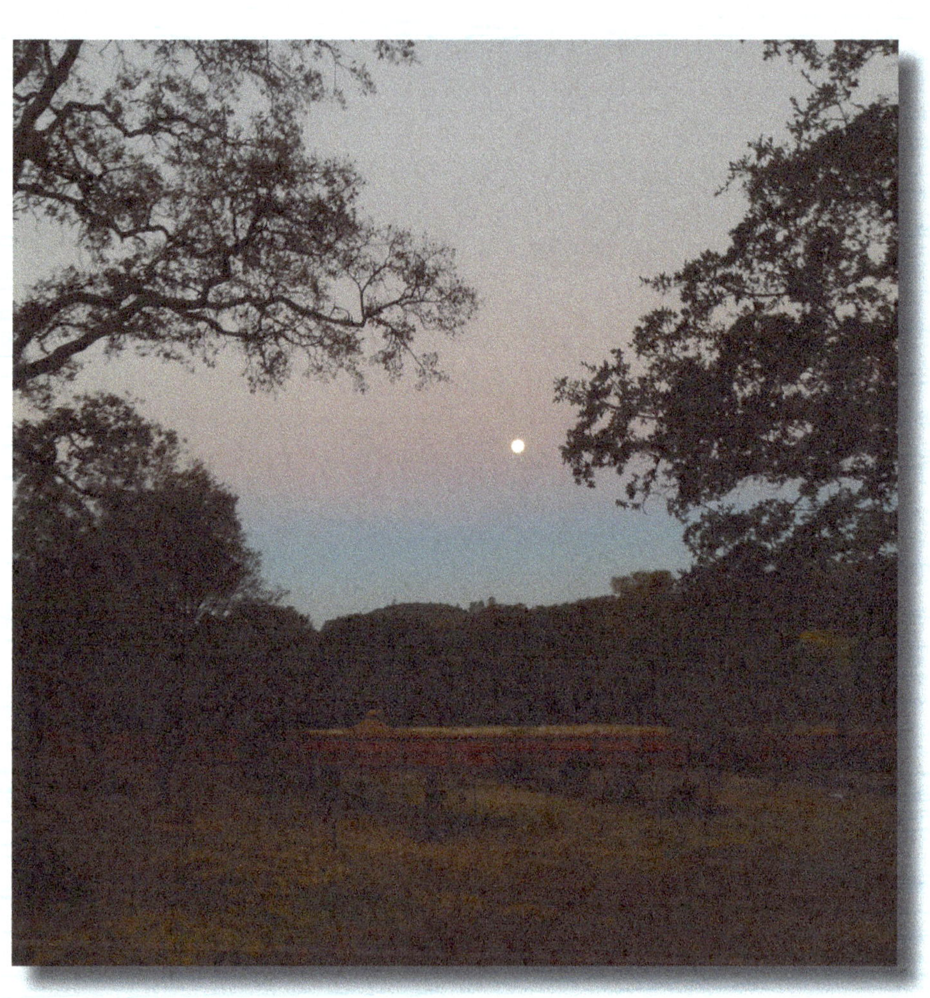

I found a little wood duck

Very newly born

While walking with my puppies

Early in the morn

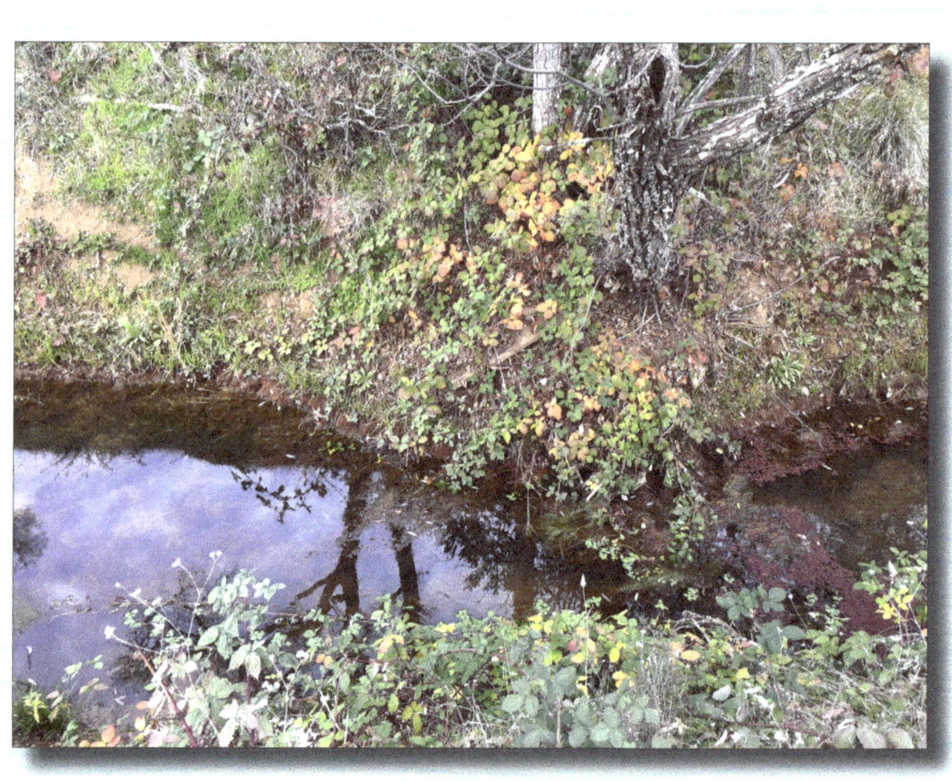

I heard a little peeping
But couldn't see the bird
Searching brambles by a stream
I saw what had occurred

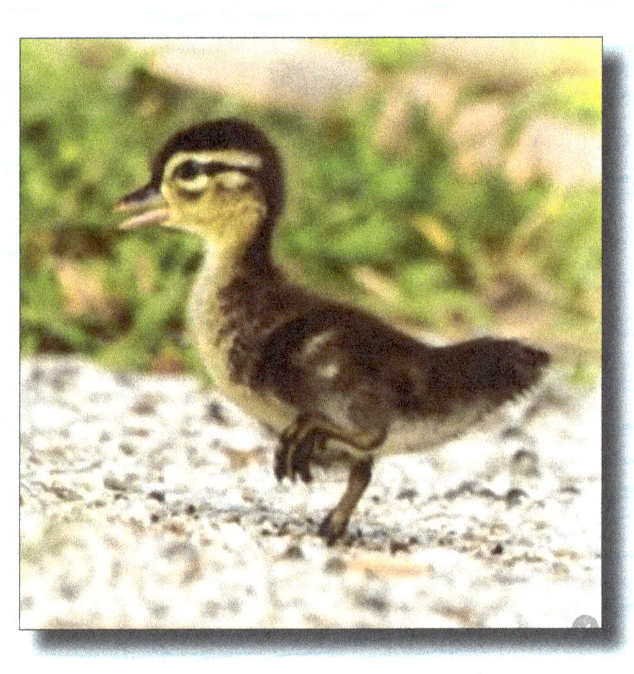

The tiny duck had caught a foot

A thorn was stuck right through

And hanging up side down was she

I swear all this is true

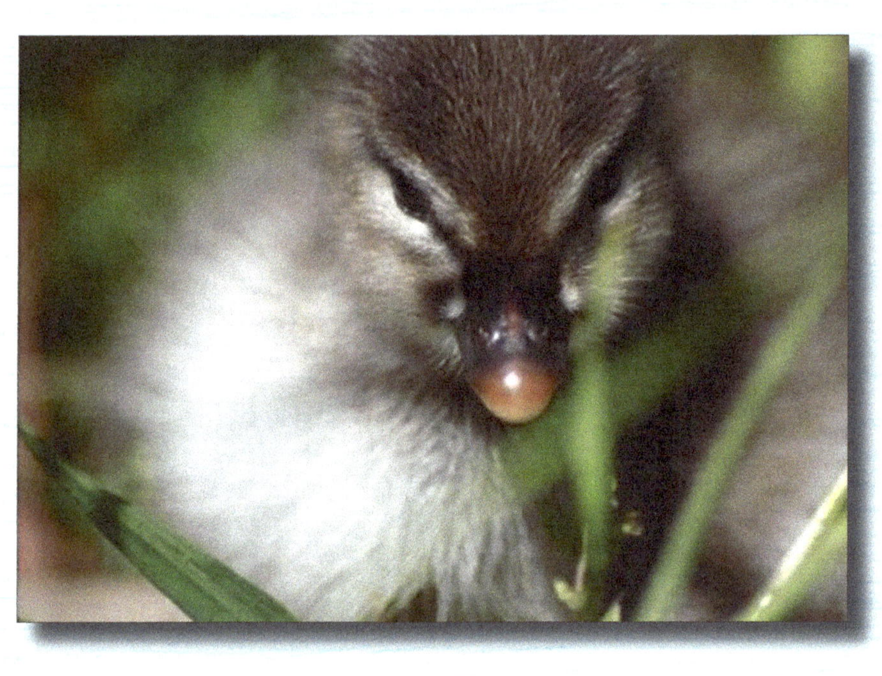

Her beak was cracked a little

Her foot was sore and torn

A frightened little bird was she

And utterly forlorn

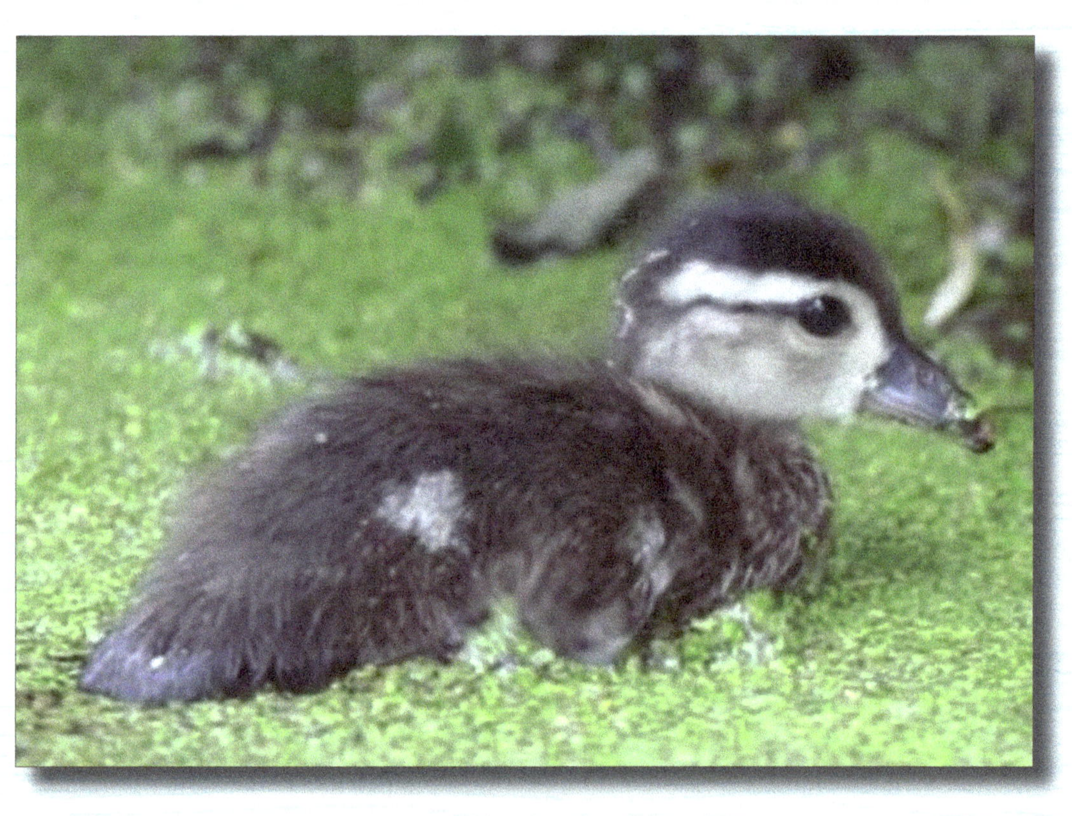

I scrambled down and freed her
And sorted out her feet
We fixed her beak with super glue
And made it clean and neat

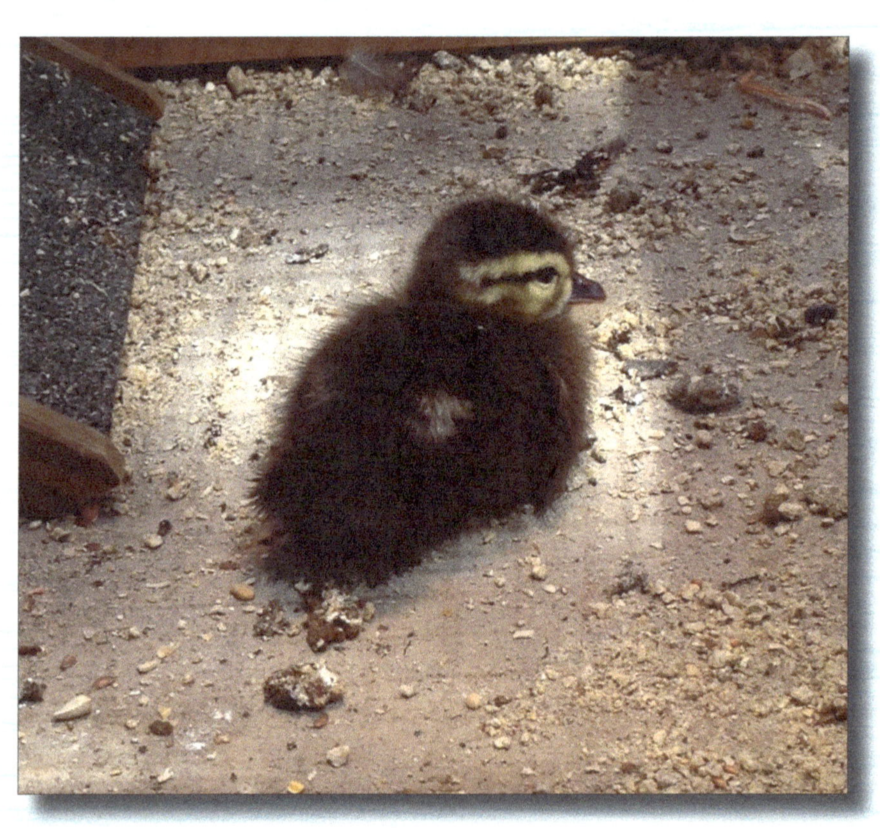

The mother duck was far away
This duckling was so small
To set her free was not to be
It wouldn't work at all!

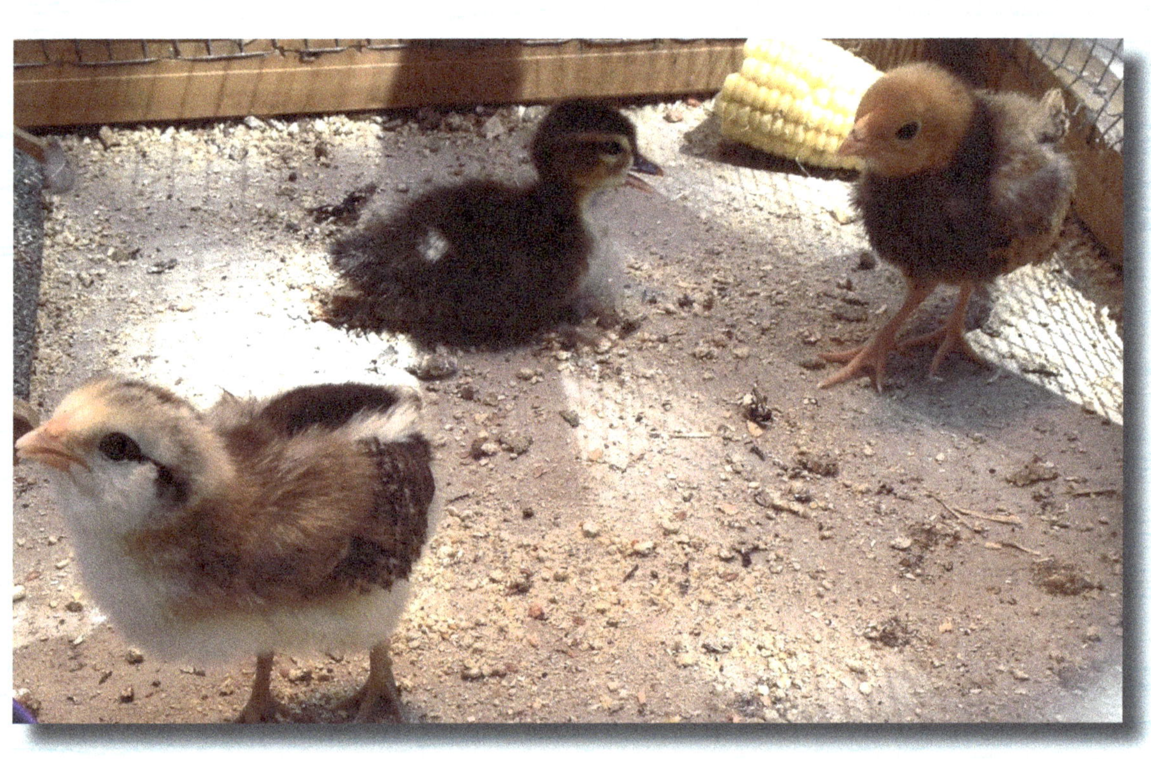

I had two chicks just two weeks old
Who had a little place
Separate in the chicken coop
For a duckling there'd be space

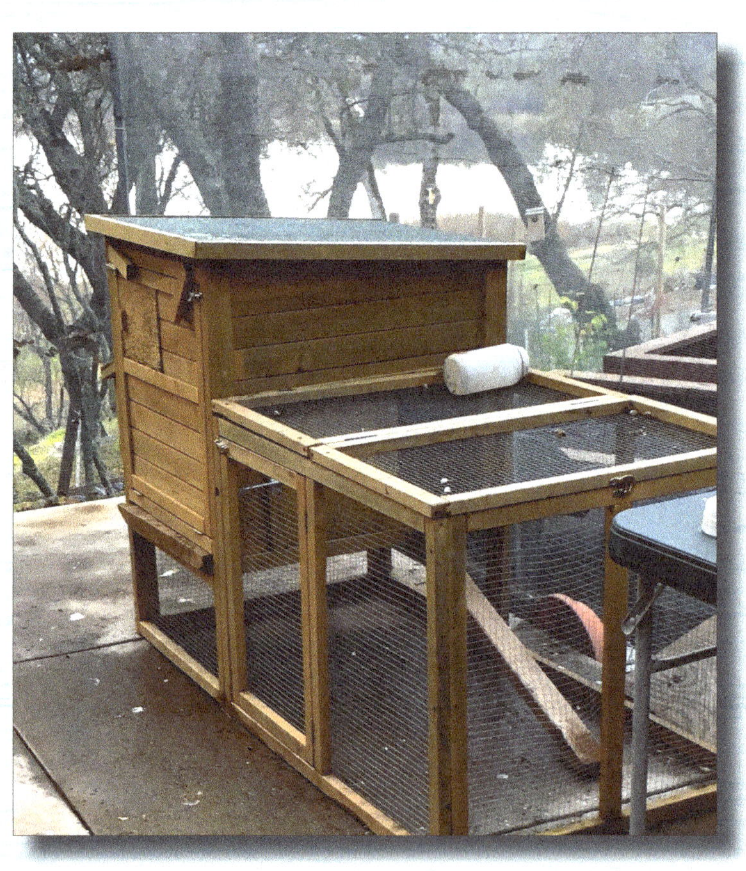

I popped her in and waited

To make sure they'd be okay

She hid out in a corner

And didn't eat all day

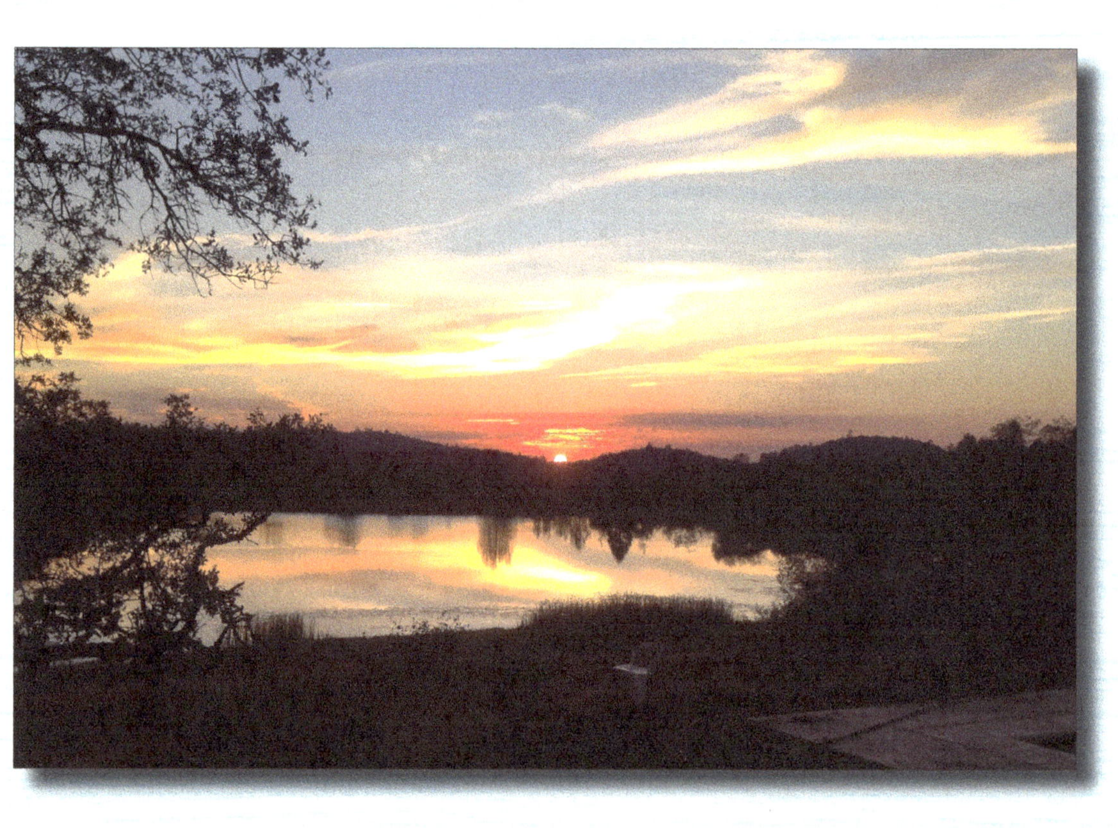

Throughout the night I worried
She was such a little duck
Would she be alive next morning?
She'd need a lot of luck

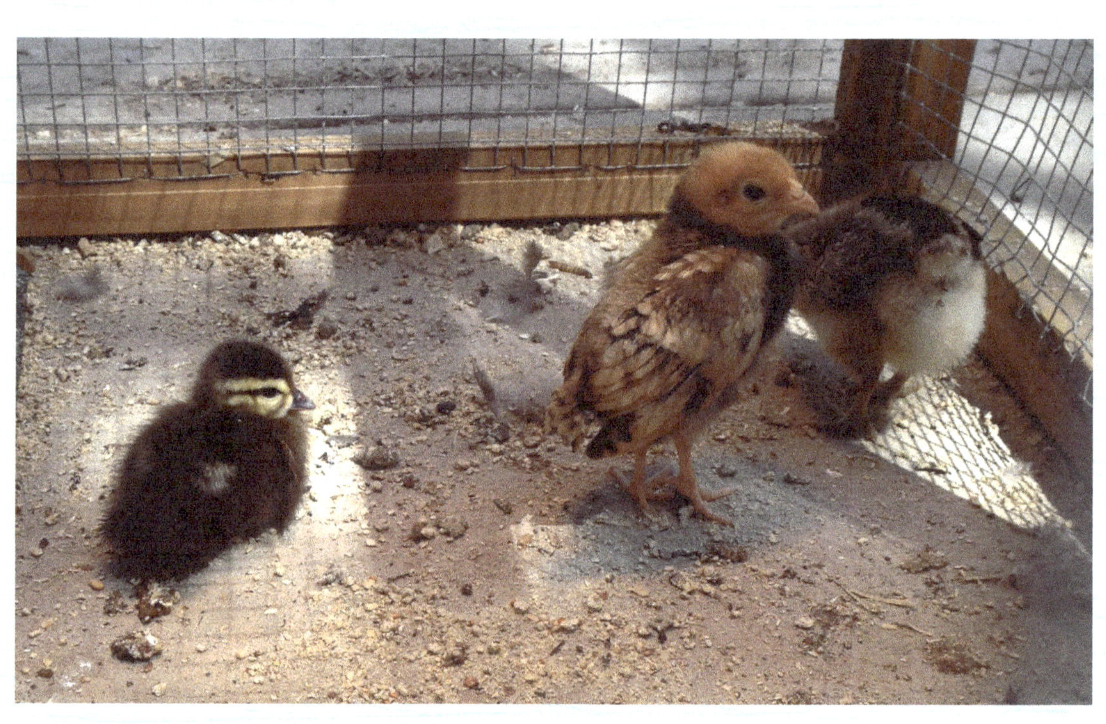

Next morning I walked over

And much to my surprise

She snuggled close to her two chicks

Although just half their size

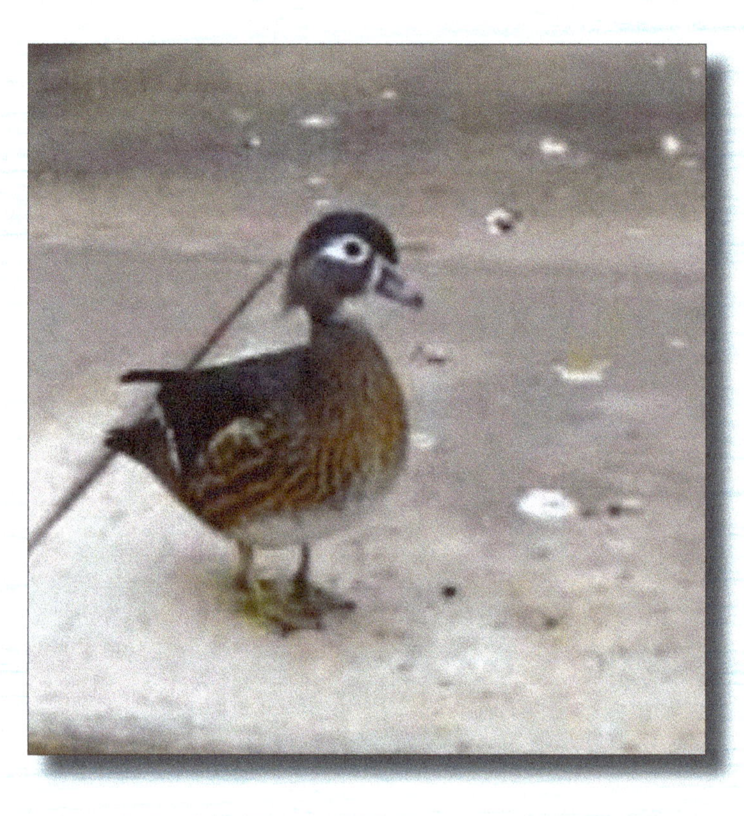

And so we called her Jenny
She grew a bit each day
And though still scared of people
With the chickens she would play

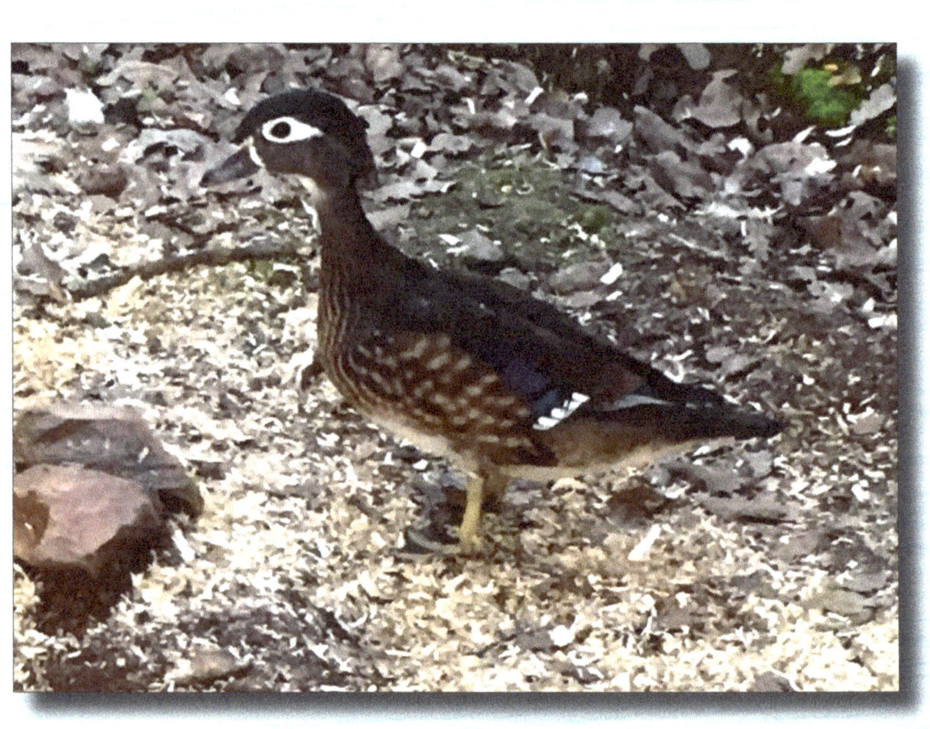

She grew up fast and learned to fly

Each morning off she'd go

Would she come back or stay away?

These things you never know

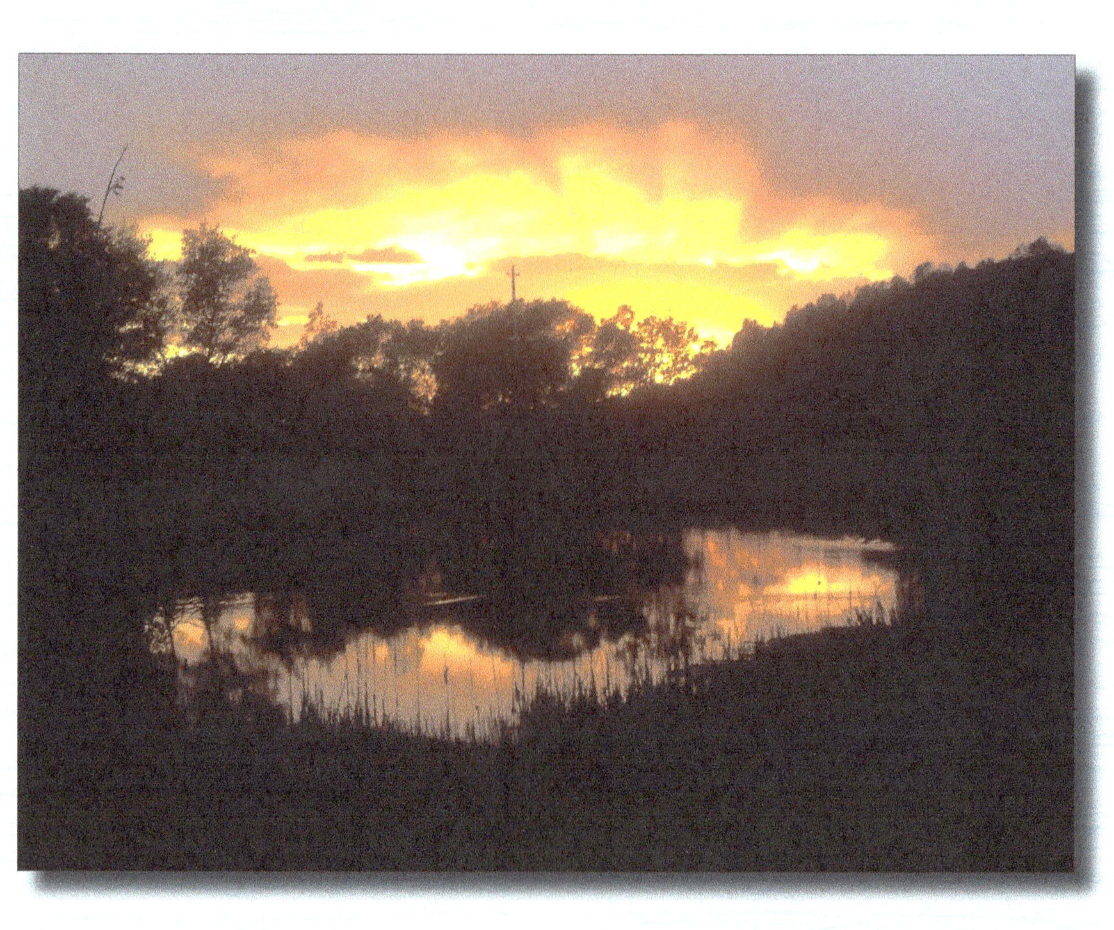

She found a flock of wild wood ducks
And with that group she'd fly
But each night as the sun went down
We'd see her in the sky

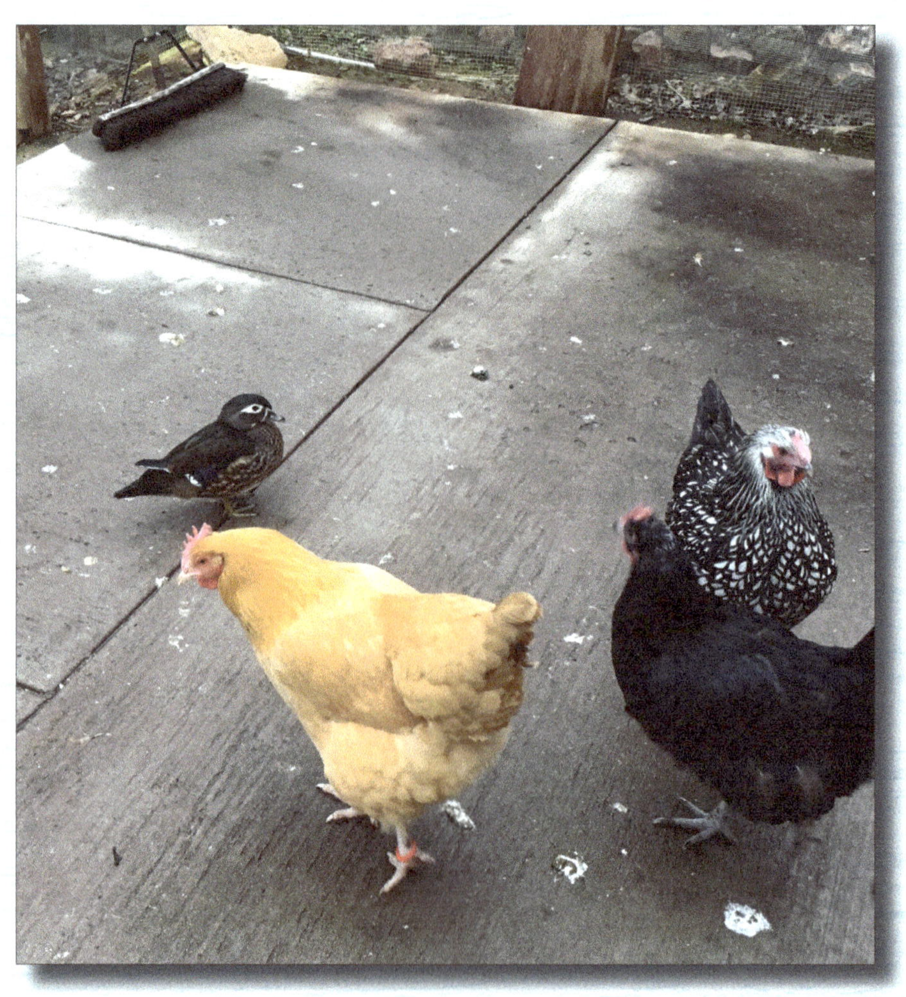

Back she'd come to her chicken pals
And inside the coop she'd go
She'd snuggle up with her two friends
Fat Anne and Little Moe

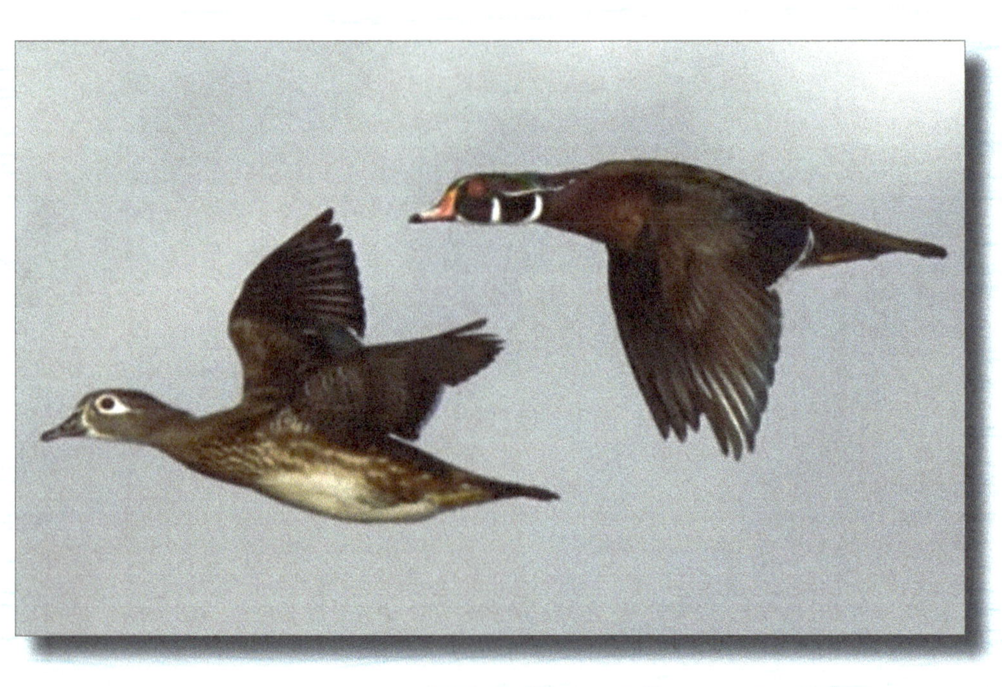

Spring came around and suddenly

Jenny had a beau

A brave young drake called Jeremy

Bright feathers all aglow

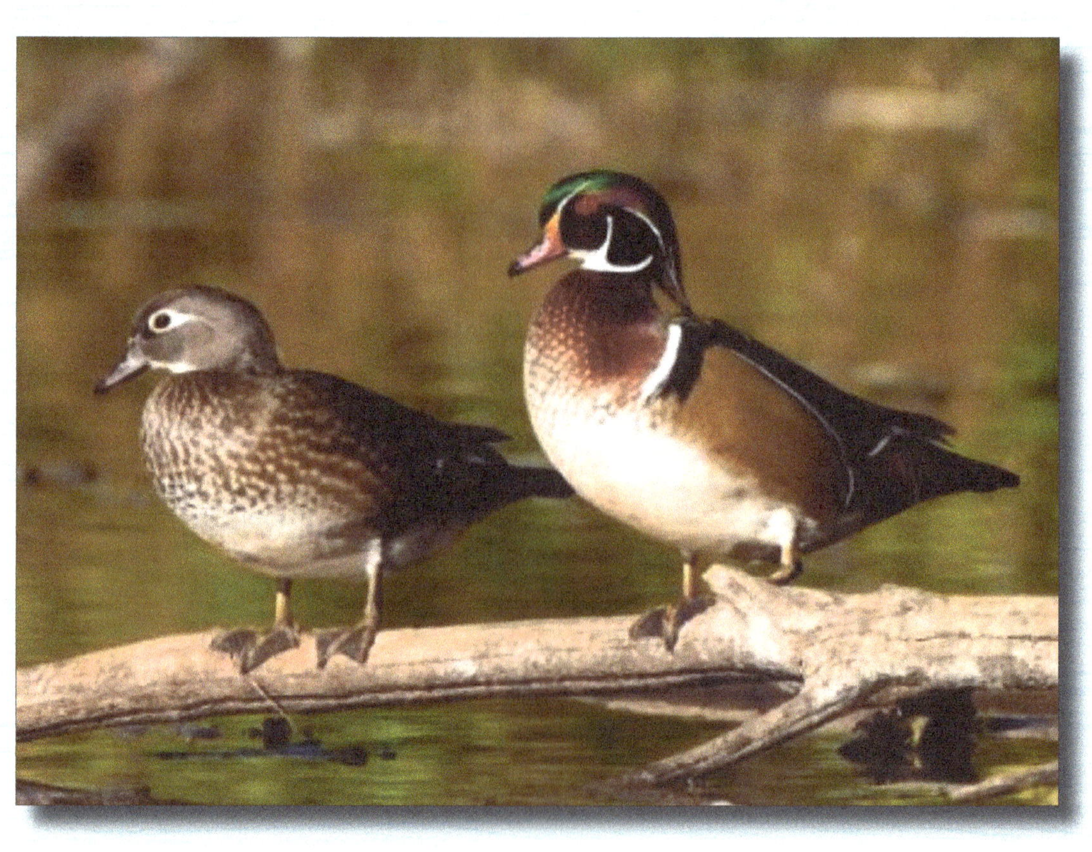

He'd call to her each morning

And follow her around

He was afraid of people

But bravely held his ground

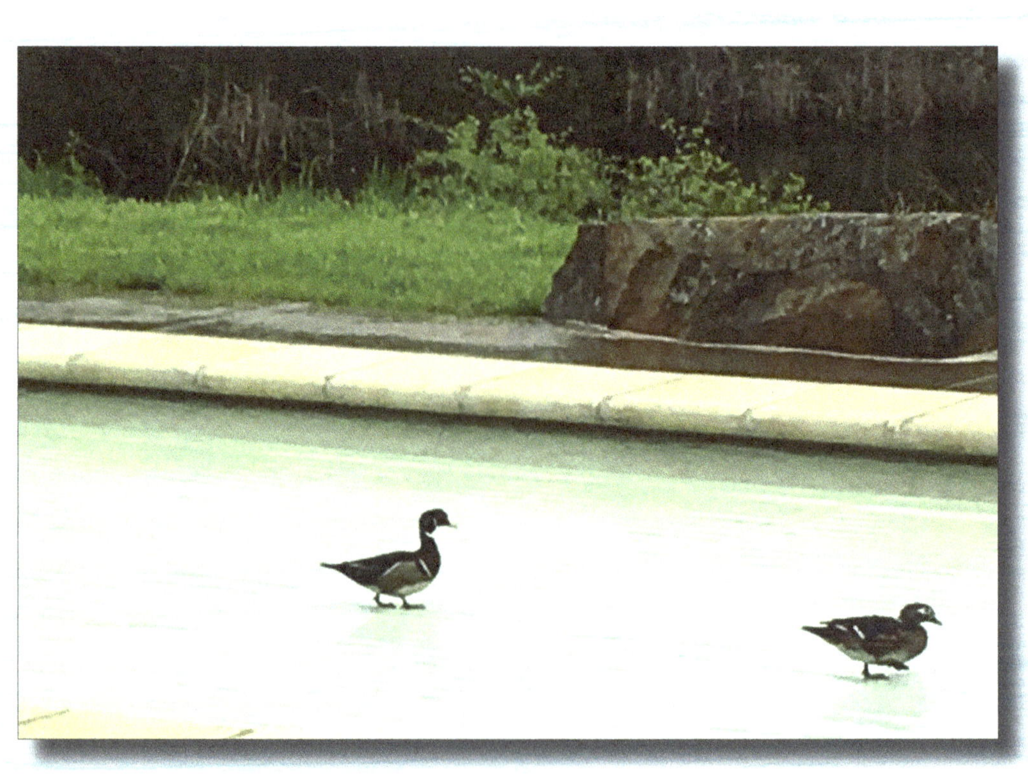

The evenings were the hardest
As Jenny would fly in
Poor Jeremy the Brave in tow
He made a dreadful din

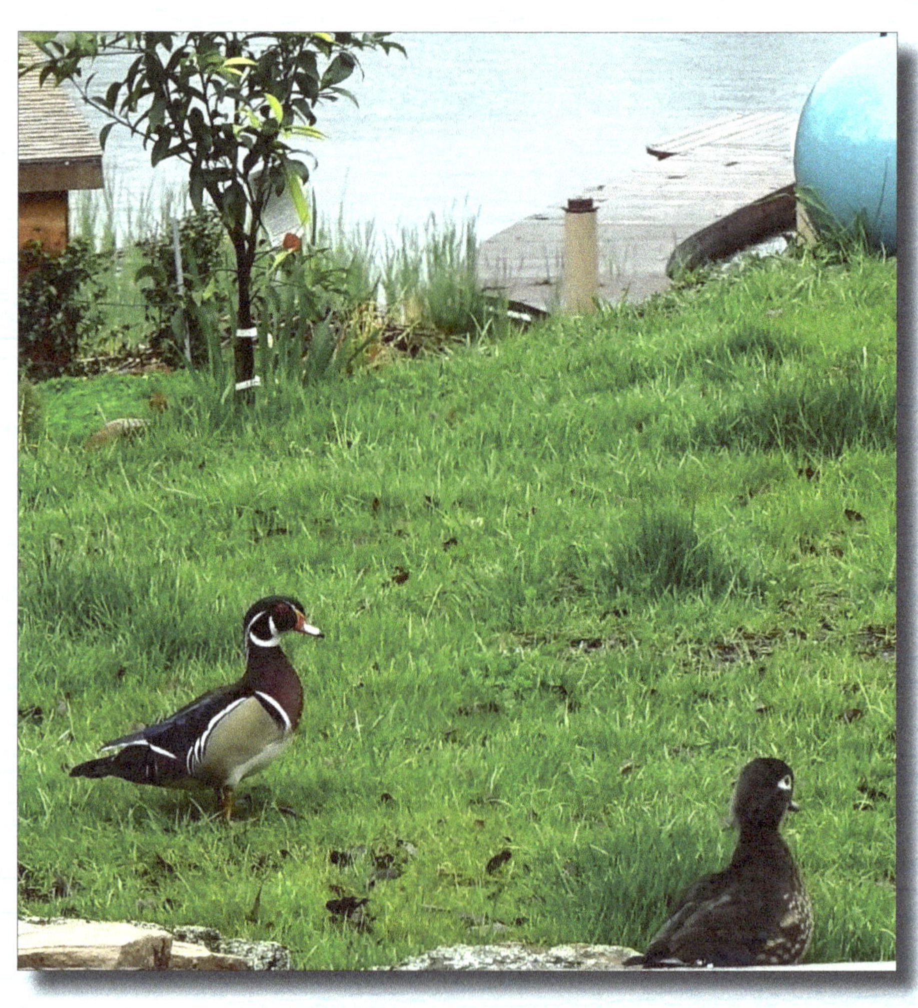

"We can't stay here!" he'd tell her
Quacking loud with fear
"Come on, come on, it's getting dark!
We must get out of here!"

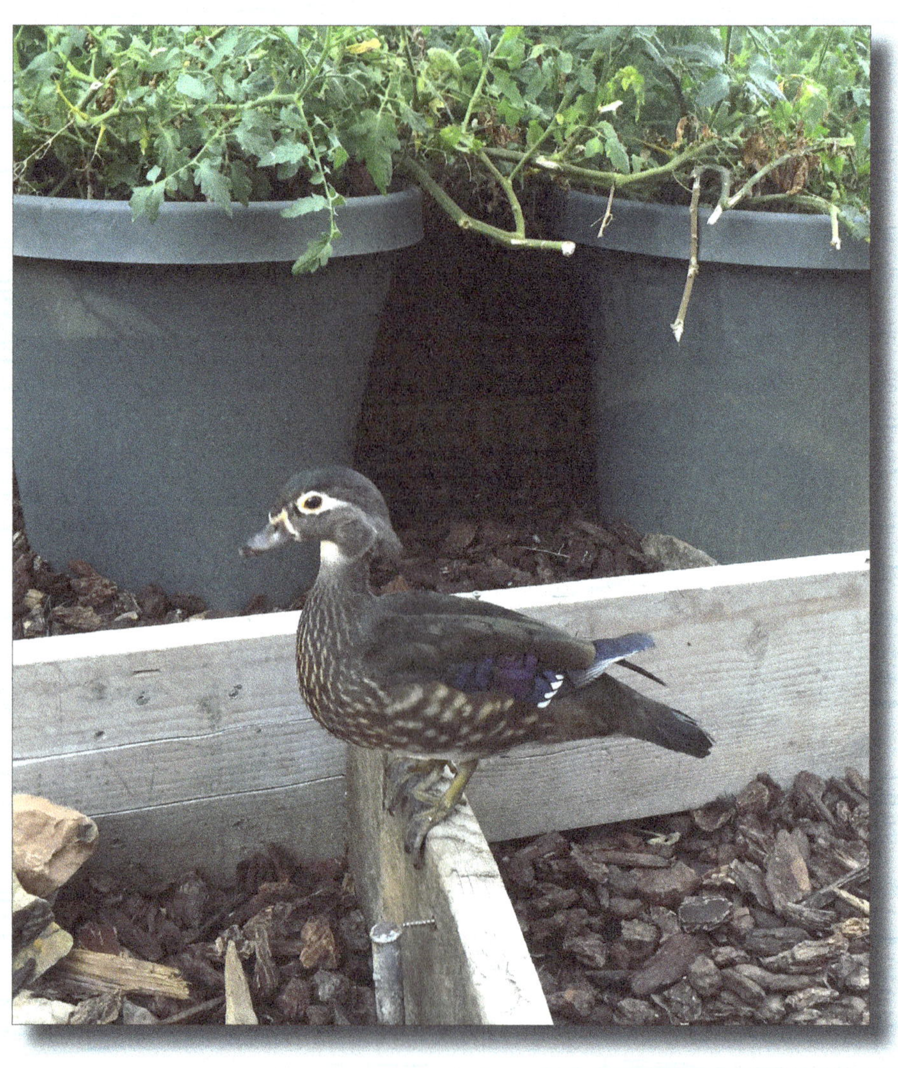

But Jenny wasn't budging
For her, this was the place
And so the hens squashed up in there
And gave Jeremy a space

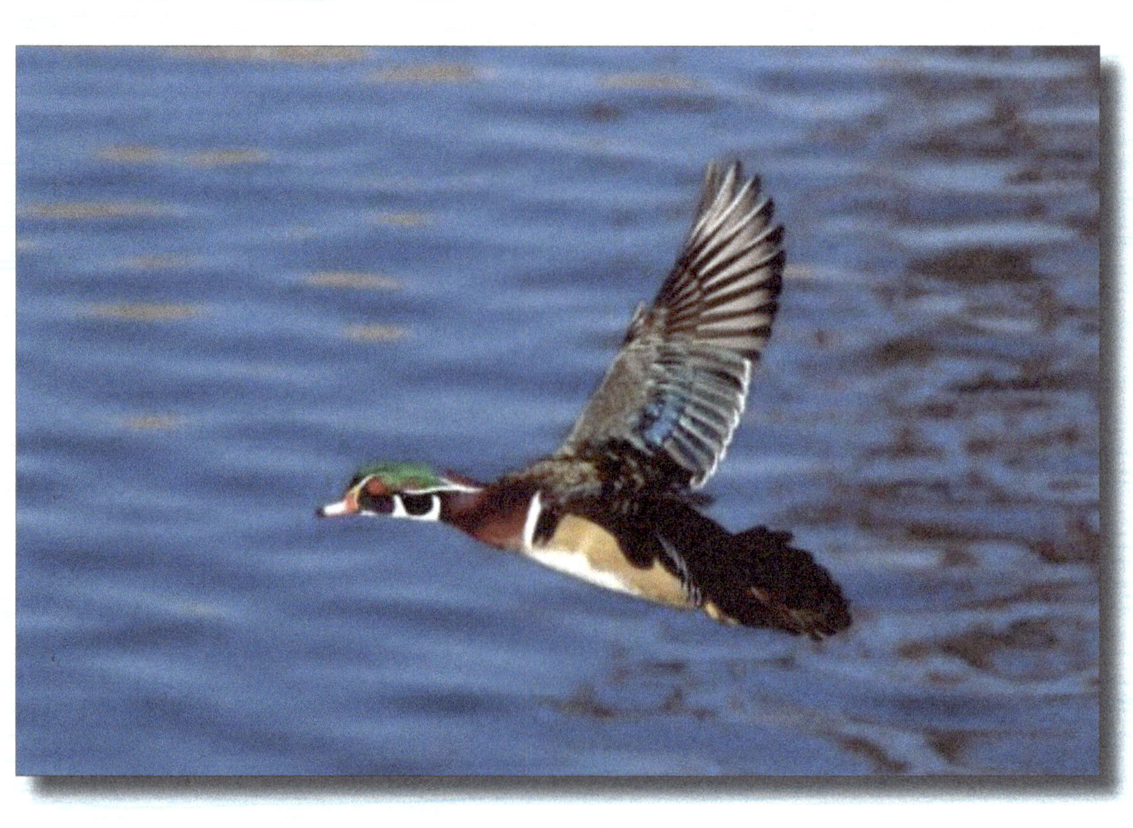

Each night I'd quietly close the door

To keep them all secure

Next day he'd quickly fly away

But he'd come back, for sure!

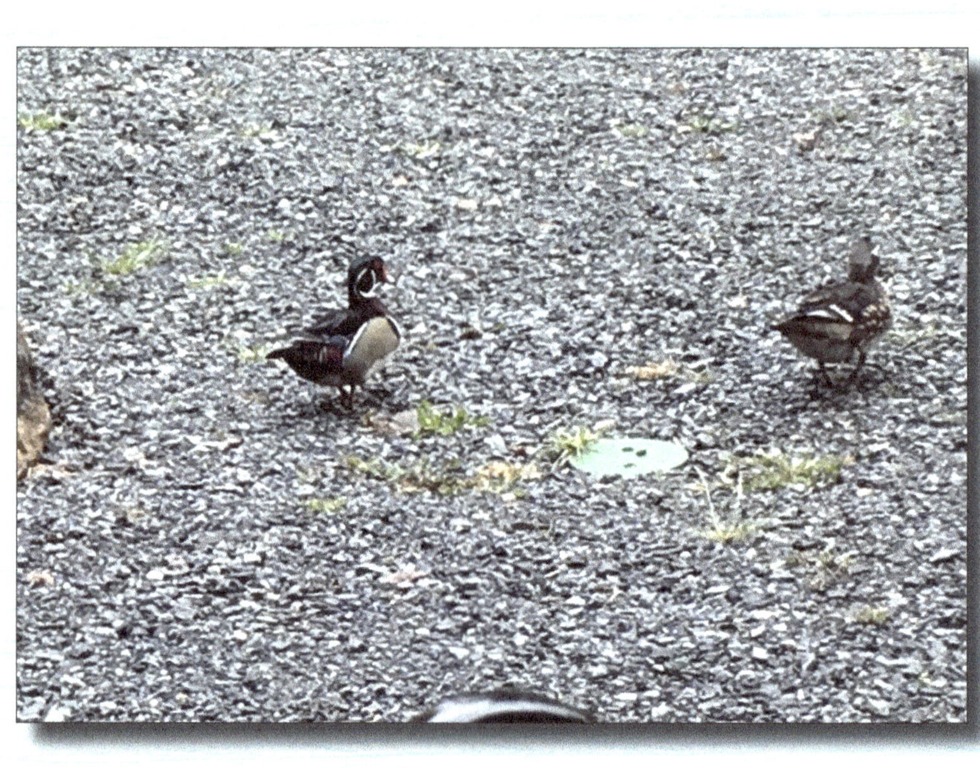

And so for several weeks that spring
We carried on that way
The ducks arrived at home each night
And then head out each day

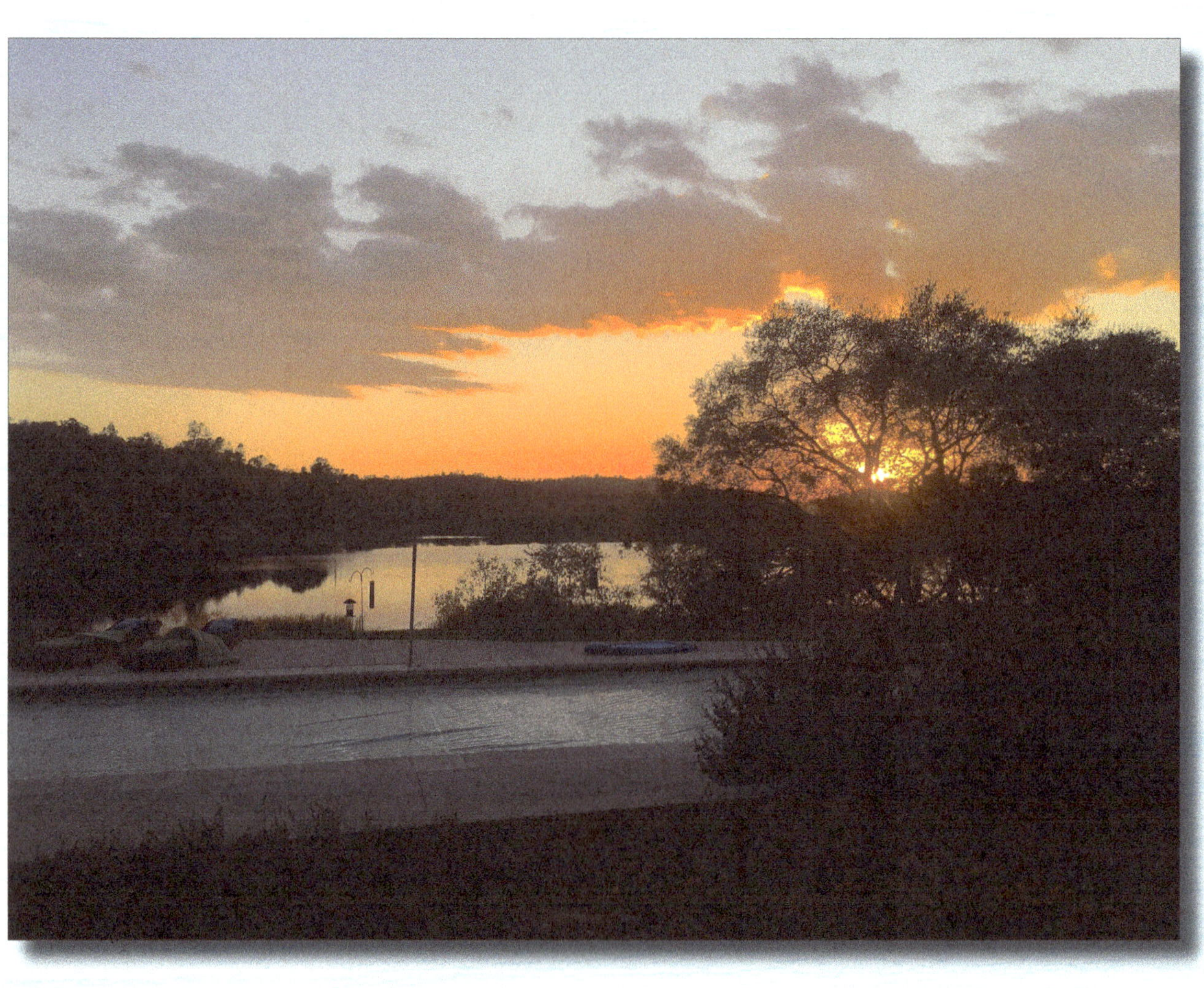

Then one day no ducks came home
No Jeremy or Jen
Had they gone for good this time?
Would I see my ducks again?

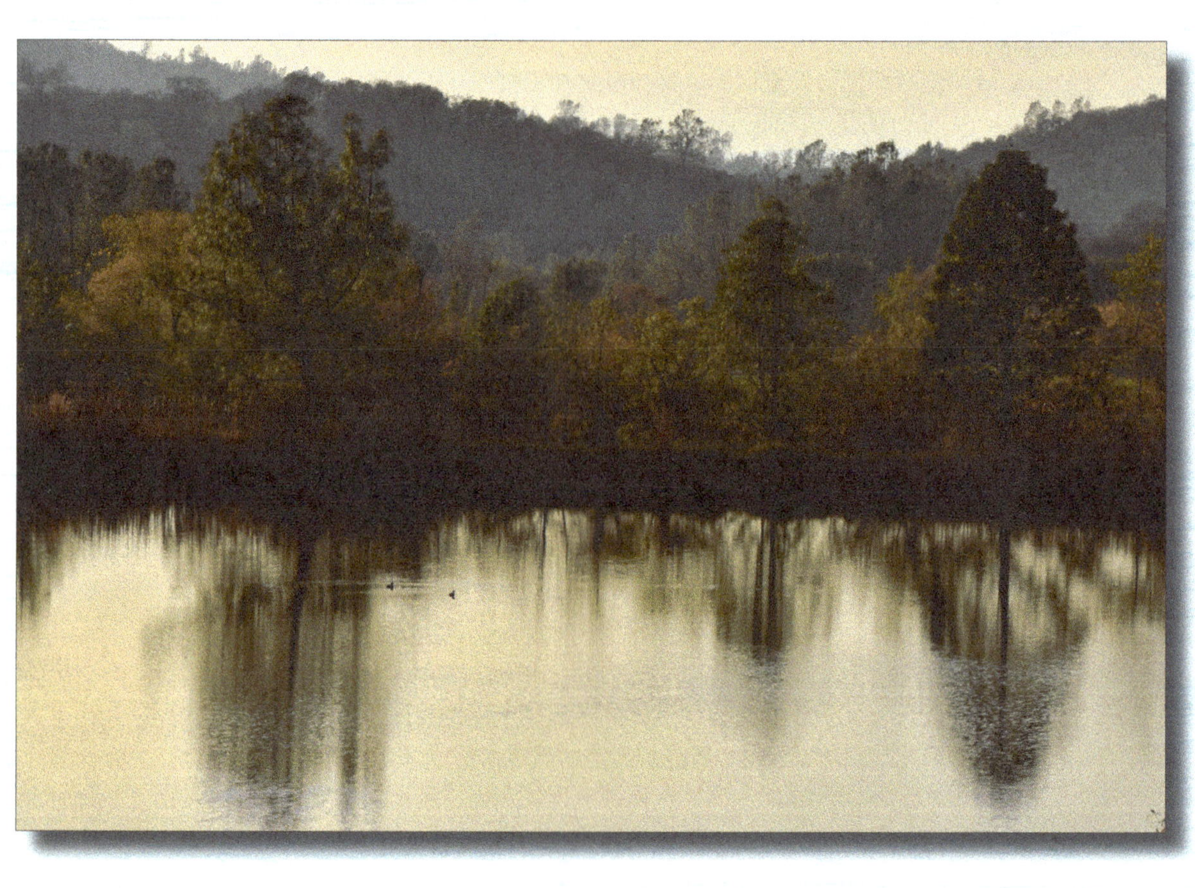

A month or so went flying by
And we didn't see our pals
But then one lovely morning
While I was feeding all the gals

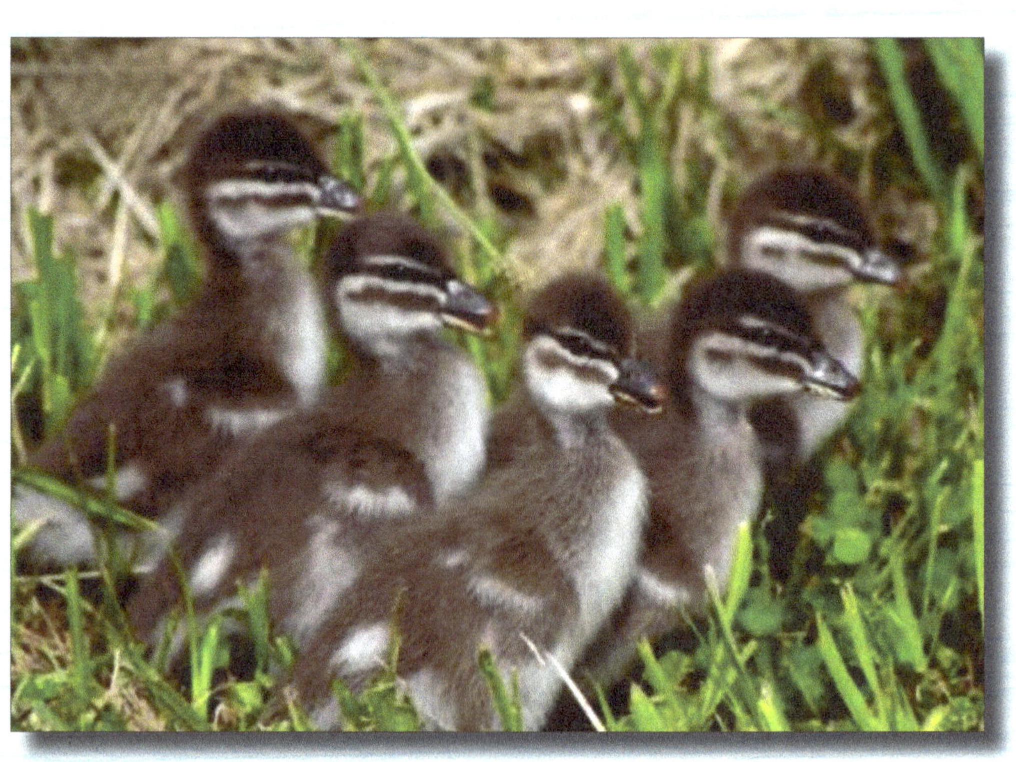

Up the hill came Jenny

Walking slowly and with care

And right behind her 12 small ducks

And then one more to spare

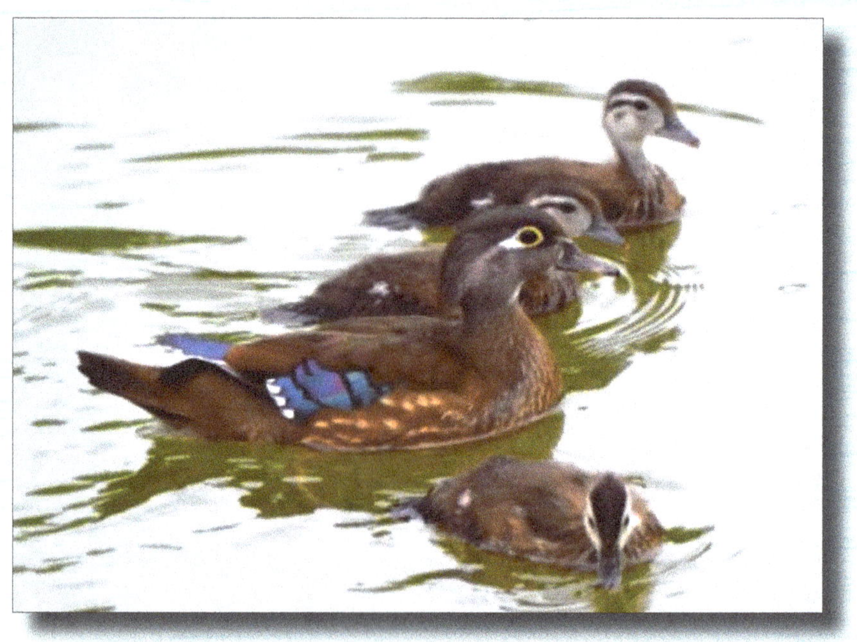

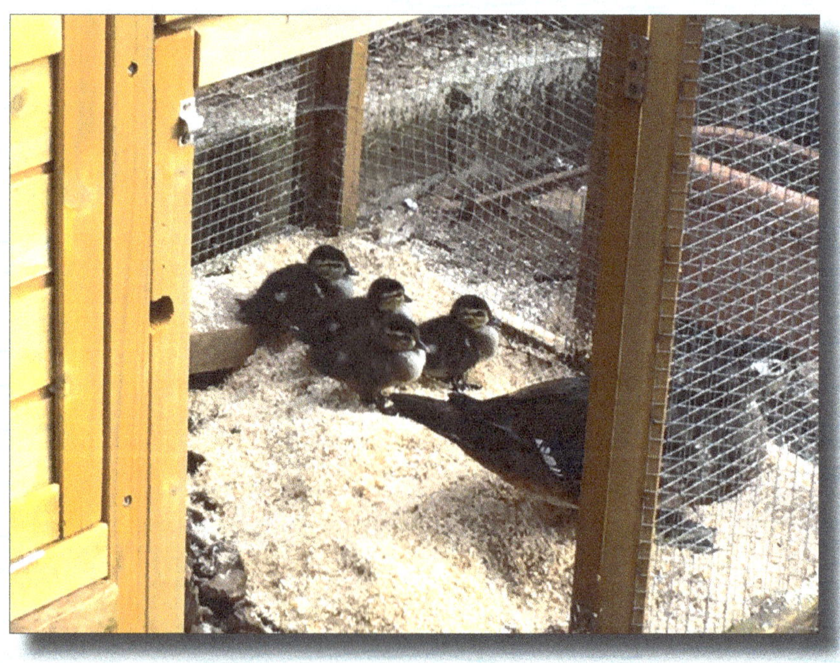

So Jenny has her family

She also has her friends

All is well In Jenny's world

And so our story ends

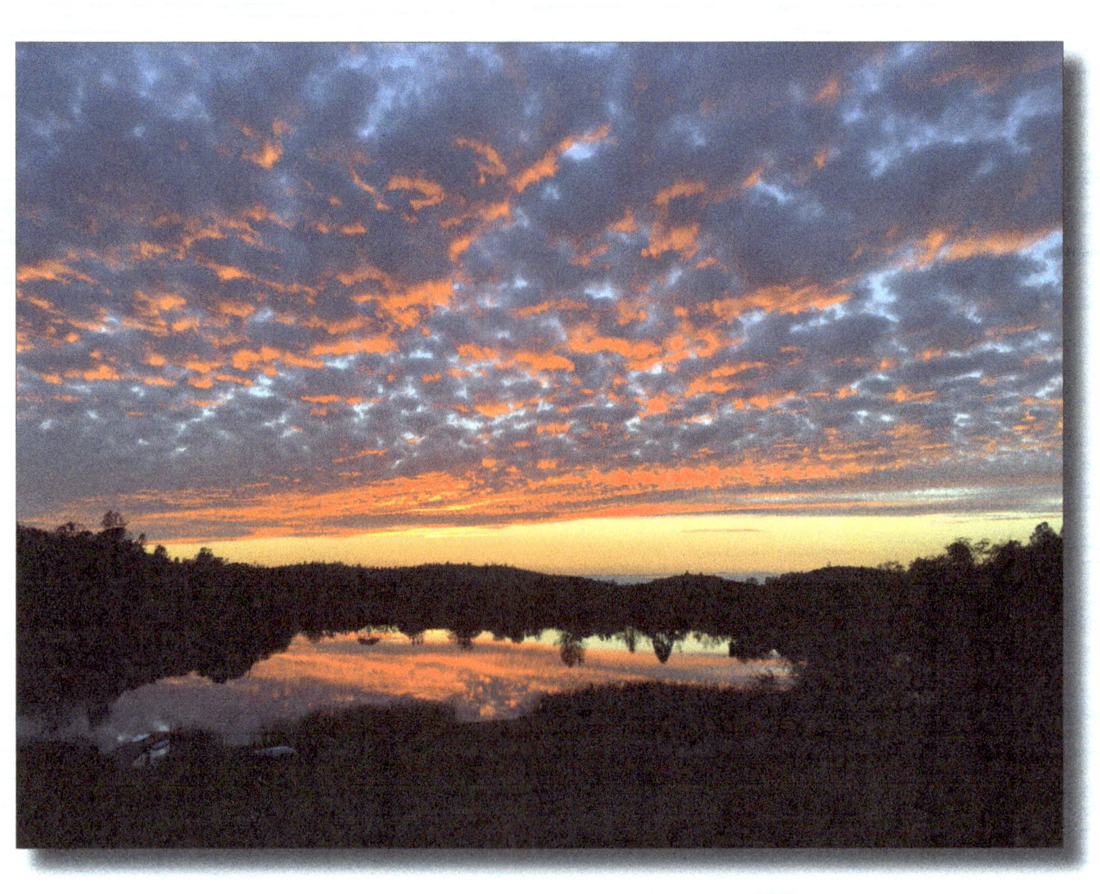

About the Author/Photographer

Jackie Caswell was born in England to English parents, but when she was three her family moved to Nairobi, Kenya for six years.

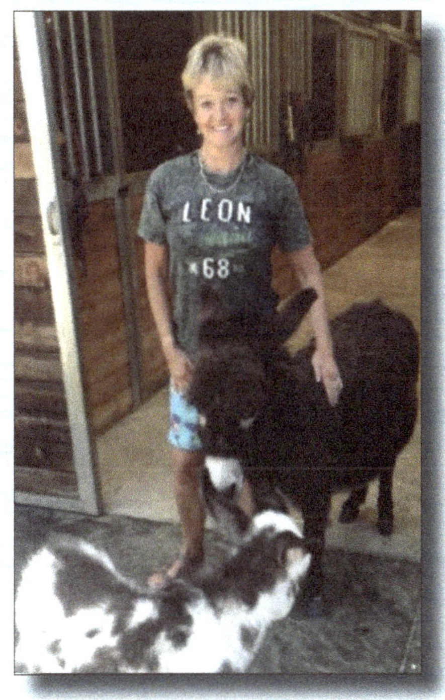

"I loved it," says Jackie. "All the birds and butterflies we saw every day, and the frogs and Chameleons that came to visit. We went on safari on a regular basis. I loved to be outside with plants and animals."

Her family later lived in Cyprus and Hong Kong, and then Jackie returned to England to earn a degree in Food Science. There she met her husband Peter. After five years living in southeast England, they moved with their two daughters to California.

When their girls left home and went to college, Jackie started a gardening company in San Francisco called Frog Hollow Gardens which she ran successfully for seven years. She also walked the *El Camino de Santiago*, which took six weeks and changed her life.

During those years, she and Peter camped on their land up in the Sierra Foothills. They moved there permanently in 2015 to live on the land and enjoy the lakes.

Jackie's mission is to turn their land into a safe haven for wildlife.

Tale of Lakewood Jenny is her first book.

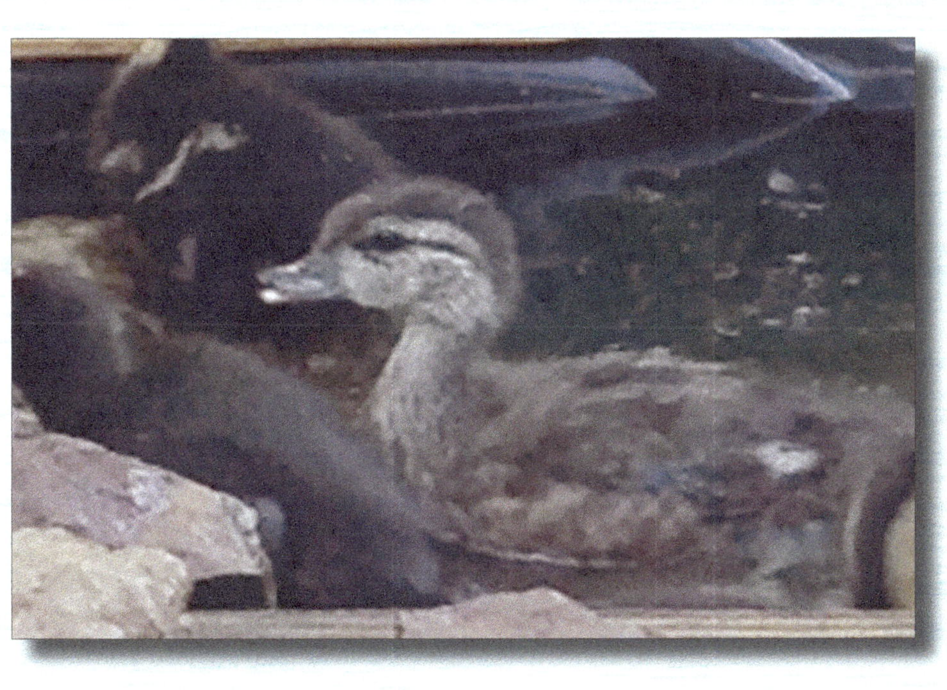

Lightning Source UK Ltd.
Milton Keynes UK
UKHW050938160820
368195UK00003B/83